SONGS FROM DEEP WATERS

Selections from the Psalms
in the New King James Version

Text by
Jill and Stuart Briscoe

Thomas Nelson Publishers
Nashville • Camden • New York

Published in Nashville, Tennessee, by Thomas Nelson, Inc., and distributed in Canada by Lawson Falle, Ltd., Cambridge, Ontario.

Text selections followed by the initials JB are by Jill Briscoe.
Text selections followed by the initials SB are by Stuart Briscoe.

ISBN 0-8407-5368-3

Printed in Singapore by Tien Wah Press (Pte.) Ltd.

SONGS FROM DEEP WATERS

Selections from the Psalms

Oh, send out Your
light and Your truth!
Let them lead me; let them
bring me to Your holy hill
And to Your
tabernacle.

Make me to hear joy and gladness,
That the bones which You have broken may rejoice.
Hide Your face from my sins,
And blot out all my iniquities.
Create in me a clean heart, O God,
And renew a right spirit within me.
Do not cast me away from Your presence,
And do not take Your Holy Spirit from me.
Restore to me the joy of Your salvation,
And uphold me with Your generous Spirit.
Then I will teach transgressors Your ways,
And sinners shall be converted to You.
Deliver me from bloodguiltiness, O God,
The God of my salvation,
And my tongue shall sing aloud of
Your righteousness. O Lord, open my lips,
And my mouth shall show forth Your praise.

Abide in the Lord

I waited patiently for the LORD;
And He inclined to me, and heard my cry.
He also brought me up out of a horrible pit,
Out of the miry clay,
And set my feet upon a rock,
And established my steps.
He has put a new song in my mouth—
Praise to our God; many will see it and fear,
And will trust in the LORD.
Blessed is that man who makes the LORD his trust,
And does not respect the proud,
Nor such as turn aside to lies.
Many, O LORD my God, are Your wonderful works
which you have done;
And Your thoughts which are toward us
Cannot be recounted to You in order;
If I would declare and speak of them,
They are more than can be numbered.
Sacrifice and offering You did not desire;
My ears You have opened;
Burnt offering and sin offering You did not require.
Then I said, "Behold, I come;
In the scroll of the Book it is written of me.
I delight to do Your will, O my God,
And Your law is within my heart."
I have proclaimed the good news of righteousness
In the great congregation;
Indeed, I do not restrain my lips,
O LORD, You Yourself know.
I have not hidden Your righteousness within my heart;
I have declared Your faithfulness and Your salvation;
I have not concealed Your lovingkindness
and Your truth from the great congregation.
Do not withhold Your tender mercies from me, O LORD;
Let Your lovingkindness and Your truth
continually preserve me.
For innumerable evils have surrounded me;
My iniquities have overtaken me. . . .
Let all those who seek You rejoice and be glad in You;
Let such as love Your salvation say continually,
"The LORD be magnified!"
But I am poor and needy; yet the LORD thinks upon me.
You are my help and my deliverer;
Do not delay, O my God.

*Every torrent has a source. There never was a
rushing stream without a quiet spring. My life
rushes and roars, but you, Lord, are my hidden
secret. I wait on You.*—SB

Trusting the Lord

Blessed is he who considers the poor;
The LORD will deliver him in the time of trouble.
The LORD will preserve him and keep him alive,
And he will be blessed on the earth;
You will not deliver him to the will of his enemies.
The LORD will strengthen him on his bed of illness;
You will sustain him on his sickbed.
I said, "LORD, be merciful to me;
Heal my soul, for I have sinned against You."
My enemies speak evil of me.
"When will he die, and his name perish?"
And if he comes to see me, he speaks vain words;
His heart gathers iniquity to itself;
When he goes out, he tells it.
All who hate me whisper together against me;
Against me they devise my hurt.
"An evil disease," they say, "clings to him.
And now that he lies down, he will rise up no more."
Even my own familiar friend in whom I trusted,
Who ate my bread, has lifted up his heel against me.
But You, O LORD, be merciful to me, and raise me up,
That I may repay them.
By this I know that You are well pleased with me,
Because my enemy does not triumph over me.
As for me, You uphold me in my integrity,
And set me before Your face forever.
Blessed be the LORD God of Israel
From everlasting to everlasting!
Amen and Amen.

Weak in the grip of sin, powerless in the face of slander, I feel the pain of those similarly afflicted. I share with them the joy of Your strength through trusting weakness—and we sleep content, like babies.—SB

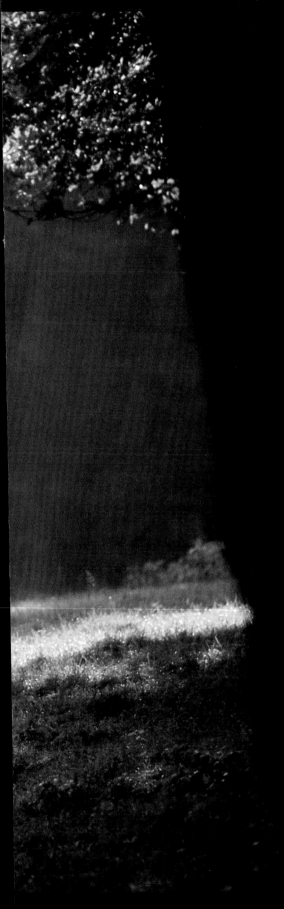

Thirst for God

As the deer pants for the water brooks,
So pants my soul for You, O God.
My soul thirsts for God, for the living God.
When shall I come and appear before God?
My tears have been my food day and night,
While they continually say to me,
"Where is your God?"
When I remember these things,
I pour out my soul within me.
For I used to go with the multitude;
I went with them to the house of God,
With the voice of joy and praise,
With a multitude that kept a pilgrim feast.
Why are you cast down, O my soul?
And why are you disquieted within me?
Hope in God, for I shall yet praise Him
For the help of His countenance.
O my God, my soul is cast down within me;
Therefore I will remember You
from the land of the Jordan,
And from the heights of Hermon, from the Hill Mizar.
Deep calls unto deep at the noise of Your waterfalls;
All Your waves and billows have gone over me.
The Lord will command His lovingkindness
in the daytime,
And in the night His song shall be with me—
A prayer to the God of my life.
I will say to God my Rock,
"Why have You forgotten me?
Why do I go mourning because of
the oppression of the enemy?"
As with a breaking of my bones,
My enemies reproach me,
While they say to me all day long,
"Where is your God?"
Why are you cast down, O my soul?
And why are you disquieted within me?
Hope in God; For I shall yet praise Him,
The help of my countenance and my God.

The best prescription for depression is to remember past blessings—and the joy of fellowship to bring to mind the order of creation—and remember God is in control. Confidence comes from remembering—AND PANTING AFTER GOD!—JB

God My Stronghold

Vindicate me, O God,
And plead my cause against an ungodly nation;
Oh, deliver me from the deceitful and unjust man!
For You are the God of my strength;
Why do You cast me off?
Why do I go mourning because of the oppression
of the enemy?
Oh, send out Your light and Your truth!
Let them lead me;
Let them bring me to Your holy hill
And to Your tabernacle.
Then I will go to the altar of God,
To God my exceeding joy;
And on the harp I will praise You,
O God, my God.
Why are you cast down, O my soul?
And why are you disquieted within me?
Hope in God;
For I shall yet praise Him,
The help of my countenance and my God.

*Going to church will not bring us joy and
delight—*
Going to God will!
Going to God when we go to church—
will hush a disturbed soul
into sweet, submissive gratitude.—JB

From PSALM 44

The Victory Comes

We have heard with our ears, O God,
Our fathers have told us,
What deed You did in their days, in days of old:
How You drove out the nations with Your hand,
But them You planted;
How You afflicted the peoples, and cast them out.
For they did not gain possession of the land
by their own sword,
Nor did their own arm save them;
But it was Your right hand, Your arm,
and the light of Your countenance,
Because You favored them.
You are my King, O God;
Command victories for Jacob.
Through You we will push down our enemies;
Through Your name we will trample those
who rise up against us.
For I will not trust in my bow,
Nor shall my sword save me.
But You have saved us from our enemies,
And have put to shame those who hated us.
In God we boast all day long,
And praise Your name forever.

[verses 1–8]

*You, O Lord, create mountains—I climb them.
You make the fields—I just till the land. I fight
the battles, but you give the victories. It was
always like this—and it ever will be.*—SB

17

Rise Up and Help Us

But You have cast us off and put us to shame,
And You do not go out with our armies.
You make us turn back from the enemy,
And those who hate us have taken spoil for themselves.
You have given us up like sheep intended for food,
And have scattered us among the nations.
You sell Your people for naught,
And are not enriched by their price.
You make us a reproach to our neighbors,
A scorn and a derision to those all around us.
You make us a byword among the nations,
A shaking of the head among the peoples.
My dishonor is continually before me,
And the shame of my face has covered me,
Because of the voice of him who reproaches
and reviles,
Because of the enemy and the avenger.
All this has come upon us;
But we have not forgotten You,
Nor have we dealt falsely with Your covenant.
Our heart has not turned back,
Nor have our steps departed from Your way;
But You have severely broken us
in the place of jackals,
And covered us with the shadow of death.
If we had forgotten the name of our God,
Or stretched out our hands to a foreign god,
Would not God search this out?
For He knows the secrets of the heart.
Yet for Your sake we are killed all day long;
We are accounted as sheep for the slaughter.
Awake! Why do You sleep, O Lord?
Arise! Do not cast us off forever.
Why do You hide Your face,
And forget our affliction and our oppression?
For our soul is bowed down to the dust;
Our body clings to the ground.
Arise for our help,
And redeem us for Your mercies' sake.

[verses 9–26]

*Gloom hangs like a mist, coldness shrouds the
soul like a blanket of snow. Bleak trees of
dismay tower gauntly over life. Pierce the
gloom with your radiance, O Lord, and like the
dawn banish the darkness of night.*—SB

The Glory of a King

My heart is overflowing with a good theme;
I recite my composition concerning the King;
My tongue is the pen of a ready writer.
You are fairer than the sons of men;
Grace is poured upon Your lips. . . .
Your throne, O God, is forever and ever; a scepter
of righteousness is the scepter of Your kingdom.
You love righteousness and hate wickedness;
Therefore God, Your God, has anointed You
With the oil of gladness
more than Your companions.
All Your garments are scented with myrrh
and aloes and cassia, out of the ivory palaces,
by which they have made You glad.
Kings' daughters are among Your honorable
women; at Your right hand stands the queen
in gold from Ophir.
Listen, O daughter, consider and incline your ear;
Forget your own people also,
and your father's house;
So the King will greatly desire your beauty;
Because He is your Lord, worship Him.
And the daughter of Tyre will be there with a gift
The rich among the people will seek your favor.
The royal daughter is all glorious within the
palace; her clothing is woven with gold. . . .
The virgins, her companions who follow her,
shall be brought to You.
With gladness and rejoicing they shall be brough
They shall enter the King's palace.
Instead of Your fathers shall be Your sons,
Whom You shall make princes in all the earth.
I will make Your name to be remembered
in all generations; therefore
the people shall praise You forever and ever.

*My heart spills over with the right
philosophy,
My King is the beginning and the end
of my beliefs.
My tongue writes this message on the
minds of men—
winging my prayers in the direction
of closed minds.
I write about the glory of a God who
got up off His throne and became
a little child!—JB*

He also brought me up
out of a horrible pit,
Out of the miry clay,
And set my feet upon a rock,
And established my steps.
He has put a new song in my mouth—
Praise to our God.

Lord of the Elements

God is our refuge and strength,
A very present help in trouble.
Therefore we will not fear,
Though the earth be removed,
And though the mountains be carried
into the midst of the sea;
Though its waters roar and be troubled,
Though the mountains shake with its swelling.   Selah
There is a river whose streams shall make glad
the city of God,
The holy place of the tabernacle of the Most High.
God is in the midst of her, she shall not be moved;
God shall help her, just at the break of dawn.
The nations raged, the kingdoms were moved;
He uttered His voice, the earth melted.
The LORD of hosts is with us;
The God of Jacob is our refuge.   Selah
Come, behold the works of the LORD,
Who has made desolations in the earth.
He makes wars cease to the end of the earth;
He breaks the bow and cuts the spear in two;
He burns the chariot in the fire.
Be still, and know that I am God;
I will be exalted among the nations,
I will be exalted in the earth!
The LORD of hosts is with us;
The God of Jacob is our refuge.   Selah

*When your world falls apart God will hold
you together. God is stable and sure.
He will steady you when the ground shakes—
He will speak and make sense of confusion.
Dawn will break and God's sun will light up
your world—
you'll see!—JB*

The Lord of All Nations

Oh, clap your hands, all you peoples!
Shout to God with the voice of triumph!
For the LORD Most High is awesome;
He is a great King over all the earth.
He will subdue the peoples under us,
And the nations under our feet.
He will choose our inheritance for us,
The excellence of Jacob whom He loves.   Selah
God has gone up with a shout,
The LORD with the sound of a trumpet.
Sing praises to God, sing praises!
Sing praises to our King, sing praises!
For God is the King of all the earth;
Sing praises with understanding.
God reigns over the nations;
God sits on His holy throne.
The princes of the people have gathered together,
The people of the God of Abraham.
For the shields of the earth belong to God;
He is greatly exalted.

There's an awesomeness about You, Lord, which can make the loftiest monarch humble himself before You. Yet there is warmth about You, which draws the smallest child to your side. Truly all the peoples of the nations can respond to You.—SB

The City of the Lord

Great is the LORD, and greatly to be praised
In the city of our God, in His holy mountain.
Beautiful in elevation, the joy of the whole earth,
Is Mount Zion on the sides of the north,
The city of the great King.
God is in her palaces; He is known as her refuge.
For behold, the kings assembled,
They passed by together.
They saw it, and so they marveled;
They were troubled, they hastened away.
Fear took hold of them there,
And pain, as of a woman in travail,
As when You break the ships of Tarshish
With an east wind.
As we have heard, so we have seen
In the city of the LORD of hosts,
In the city of our God:
God will establish it forever.   Selah
We have thought, O God, on Your lovingkindness,
In the midst of Your temple.
According to Your name, O God,
So is Your praise to the ends of the earth;
Your right hand is full of righteousness.
Let Mount Zion rejoice,
Let the daughters of Judah be glad,
Because of Your judgments.
Walk about Zion, and go all around her.
Count her towers;
Mark well her bulwarks;
Consider her palaces;
That you may tell it to the generation following.
For this is God, our God forever and ever;
He will be our guide even to death.

*There is an abiding quality to Mount Zion.
Armies have besieged her, famine and distress
have overwhelmed her, but she remains
impervious, indomitable. I stand in the valley,
looking up to her heights, and I'm reminded
that the God of Mount Zion is all powerful and
His love unfailing.—SB*

Trust the Lord—Not Your Riches

Hear this, all you peoples;
Give ear, all you inhabitants of the world.
Both low and high, rich and poor together.
My mouth shall speak wisdom, and the meditation
of my heart shall bring understanding.
I will incline my ear to a proverb;
I will disclose my dark saying on the harp.
Why should I fear in the days of evil,
When the iniquity at my heels surrounds me?
Those who trust in their wealth and boast
in the multitude of their riches,
None of them can by any means redeem his brother.
Nor give to God a ransom for him—
For the redemption of their souls is costly,
And it shall cease forever—
That he should continue to live eternally,
And not see the Pit.
For he sees that wise men die;
Likewise the fool and the senseless person perish,
And leave their wealth to others.
Their inner thought is that their houses
will continue forever.
And their dwelling places to all generations;
They call their lands after their own names.
Nevertheless man, though in honor, does not remain;
He is like the beasts that perish.
This is the way of those who are foolish,
And of their posterity
who approve their sayings.   Selah
Like sheep they are laid in the grave;
Death shall feed on them;
The upright shall have dominion over them in the
morning;
And their beauty shall be consumed in the grave,
far from their dwelling.
But God will redeem my soul from the power
of the grave,
For He shall receive me.   Selah

The clever man must leave his books,
The wealthy man his money,
The rich their pretty homes,
The famous their fans,
The young their beauty.
Then all that will count will be God
and His power to redeem from the grave.—JB

The Lord Delights In—

The Mighty One, God the LORD,
Has spoken and called the earth
From the rising of the sun to its going down.
Out of Zion, the perfection of beauty,
God will shine forth.
Our God shall come, and shall not keep silent;
A fire shall devour before Him,
And it shall be very tempestuous all around Him.
He shall call to the heavens from above,
And to the earth, that He may judge His people:
"Gather My saints together to Me,
Those who have made a covenant with Me by sacrifice."
Let the heavens declare His righteousness.
For God Himself is Judge.   Selah
"Hear, O My people, and I will speak,
O Israel, and I will testify against you;
I am God, your God!
I will not reprove you for your sacrifices
Or your burnt offerings,
Which are continually before Me.
I will not take a bull from your house,
Nor goats out of your folds.
For every beast of the forest is Mine,
And the cattle on a thousand hills.
I know all the birds of the mountains,
And the wild beasts of the field are Mine.
"If I were hungry, I would not tell you;
For the world is Mine, and all its fullness.
Will I eat the flesh of bulls,
Or drink the blood of goats?
Offer to God thanksgiving,
And pay your vows to the Most High.
Call upon Me in the day of trouble;
I will deliver you, and you shall glorify Me."

We offer God plenty of "pleases" and plenty
of "sorrys." He likes to hear us offer
"thank yous" once in a while.
We are such thankless creatures.
One leper out of ten returned to thank
Jesus for his healing.
Our Lord asked, "Where are the nine?"
The Lord delights in thank offerings!—JB

From PSALM 51

The Lord Renews Your Spirit

Have mercy upon me, O God,
According to Your lovingkindness;
According to the multitude of Your tender mercies,
Blot out my transgressions.
Wash me thoroughly from my iniquity,
And cleanse me from my sin.
For I acknowledge my transgressions,
And my sin is ever before me.
Against You, You only, have I sinned,
And done this evil in Your sight—
That You may be found just when You speak,
And blameless when You judge.
Behold, I was brought forth in iniquity,
And in sin my mother conceived me.
Behold, You desire truth in the inward parts,
And in the hidden part You will make me
to know wisdom.
Purge me with hyssop, and I shall be clean;
Wash me, and I shall be whiter than snow.
Make me to hear joy and gladness,
That the bones which You have broken may rejoice.
Hide Your face from my sins,
And blot out all my iniquities.
Create in me a clean heart, O God,
And renew a steadfast spirit within me.
Do not cast me away from Your presence,
And do not take Your Holy Spirit from me.
Restore to me the joy of Your salvation,
And uphold me with Your generous Spirit.
Then I will teach transgressors Your ways,
And sinners shall be converted to You.
Deliver me from bloodguiltiness, O God,
The God of my salvation,
And my tongue shall sing aloud of Your righteousness.
O Lord, open my lips, and my mouth shall show forth
Your praise.
For You do not desire sacrifice, or else
I would
give it; You do not delight in burnt offering.
The sacrifices of God are a broken spirit,
A broken and a contrite heart—
These, O God, You will not despise.

[verses 1–17]

*As surely as the softness of spring will banish
the harshness of winter, and the coldness of the
snow will provide the freshness of water, so the
grace and mercy of God produce a renewal of
Spirit to those who truly repent and seek His
face.—SB*

Trust God's Unfailing Love

Why do you boast in evil, O mighty man?
The goodness of God endures continually.
Your tongue devises destruction,
Like a sharp razor, working deceitfully.
You love evil more than good,
And lying rather than speaking righteousness.   Selah
You love all devouring words, you deceitful tongue.
God shall likewise destroy you forever;
He shall take you away, and pluck you
out of your dwelling place,
And uproot you from the land of the living.   Selah
The righteous also shall see and fear,
And shall laugh at him, saying,
"Here is the man who did not make God his strength,
But trusted in the abundance of his riches,
And strengthened himself in his wickedness."
But I am like a green olive tree in the house of God;
I trust in the mercy of God forever and ever.
I will praise You forever, because You have done it;
And in the presence of Your saints
I will wait on Your name, for it is good.

*The harsh realities of life are plain to see.
Mankind's callous indifference to God, which so
often leads to open disdain for Him, is in
evidence on every hand. I fear for those who
live like this, and I long, in my experience of
God, to present an alternative that is fresh,
attractive, and unmistakably unavoidable.*—SB

Therefore we will not fear,
Though the earth be removed,
And the mountains be carried into the midst of the sea;
Though its waters roar and be troubled,
Though the mountains shake with its swelling.

The Wise Man Seeks God

The fool has said in his heart,
"There is no God."
They are corrupt, and have done abominable iniquity;
There is none who does good.
God looks down from heaven upon the children of men,
To see if there are any who understand, who seek God.
Every one of them has turned aside;
They have together become corrupt;
There is none who does good,
No, not one.
Have the workers of iniquity no knowledge,
Who eat up my people as they eat bread,
And do not call upon God?
There they are in great fear where no fear was,
For God has scattered the bones of him who encamps against you;
You have put them to shame,
Because God has despised them.
Oh, that the salvation of Israel would come out of Zion!
When God brings back the captivity of His people,
Let Jacob rejoice and Israel be glad.

Knowledge is an accumulation of facts.
Wisdom is knowing what to do with them.
The fear of the Lord is the beginning of wisdom.
A fool can know a lot, but if he knows not God
he knows nothing of eternal worth, and his
knowledge, like his soul, shall pass away into
darkness.
God is looking for wise men!—JB

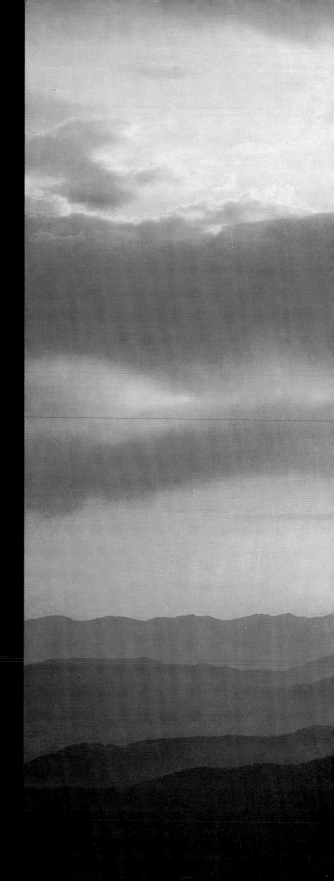

Call to God and He Saves You

Save me, O God, by Your name,
And vindicate me by Your strength.
Hear my prayer, O God;
Give ear to the words of my mouth.
For strangers have risen up against me,
And oppressors have sought after my life;
They have not set God before them.   Selah
Behold, God is my helper;
The Lord is with those who uphold my life.
He will repay my enemies for their evil.
Cut them off in Your truth.
I will freely sacrifice to You;
I will praise Your name, O LORD, for it is good.
For He has delivered me out of all trouble;
And my eye has seen its desire upon my enemies.

Samuel says, "And David made haste to get away for fear of Saul." Hounded day and night by Saul's men on one side of the mountain and he and his men on the other side, the psalmist turned to song for repose. Music soothes the nerves and calms the fears. David's songs do not always stay in minor key. A little note of praise does the soul good—like medicine!—JB

From PSALM 55

My Place of Shelter

Give ear to my prayer, O God,
And do not hide Yourself from my supplication.
Attend to me, and hear me;
I am restless in my complaint, and moan noisily,
Because of the voice of the enemy,
Because of the oppression of the wicked;
For they bring down trouble upon me,
And in wrath they hate me.
My heart is severely pained within me,
And the terrors of death have fallen upon me.
Fearfulness and trembling have come upon me,
And horror has overwhelmed me.
And I said, "Oh, that I had wings like a dove!
For then I would fly away and be at rest.
Indeed, I would wander far off,
And remain in the wilderness.   Selah
I would hasten my escape
From the windy storm and tempest."
Destroy, O Lord, and divide their tongues,
For I have seen violence and strife in the city.
Day and night they go around it on its walls;
Iniquity and trouble are also in the midst of it.
Destruction is in its midst;
Deceit and guile do not depart from its streets.
For it is not an enemy who reproaches me;
Then I could bear it.
Nor is it one who hates me who has
Magnified himself against me;
Then I could hide from him.
But it was you, a man my equal,
My companion and my acquaintance.
We took sweet counsel together,
And walked to the house of God in the throng.
[verses 1–14]

*There is a limit to my endurance, Lord. I can
only take so much, and I've almost arrived at
my breaking point. All I want to do is fly
away, escape, go to the desert place and hide.
But there is no need, for You are my refuge—to
You I can go and find that prayer has
wings.—SB*

From PSALM 55

Call to God

As for me, I will call upon God,
And the LORD shall save me.
Evening and morning and at noon
I will pray, and cry aloud,
And He shall hear my voice.
He has redeemed my soul in peace
from the battle which was against me,
For there were many against me.
God will hear, and afflict them,
Even He who abides from of old.   Selah
Because they do not change,
Therefore they do not fear God.
He has put forth his hands against those
who were at peace with him;
He has broken his covenant.
The words of his mouth
were smoother than butter,
But war was in his heart;
His words were softer than oil,
Yet they were drawn swords.
Cast your burden on the LORD,
And He shall sustain you;
He shall never permit the righteous to be moved
But You, O God, shall bring them down
to the pit of destruction;
Bloodthirsty and deceitful men shall not live out
half their days;
But I will trust in You.   [verses 16–23

*Words sometimes cut deeper than
swords. And when they are smooth
words, wounds go deeper and take longer
to heal. I want to retaliate, but instead I
meditate. Pondering the lot of those
whose words spring from hearts hardened
to You, Lord, I contemplate their fate
with sorrow and trust myself to You for
Your gracious aid.—SB*

What Can Man Do to Me?

Be merciful to me, O God, for man would
swallow me up;
Fighting all day he oppresses me.
My enemies would hound me all day,
For there are many who fight against me, O Most High.
Whenever I am afraid, I will trust in You.
In God (I will praise His word),
In God I have put my trust;
I will not fear.
What can flesh do to me?
All day they twist my words;
All their thoughts are against me for evil.
They gather together, they hide, they mark my steps,
When they lie in wait for my life.
Shall they escape by iniquity?
In anger cast down the peoples, O God!
You number my wanderings;
Put my tears into Your bottle;
Are they not in Your book?
When I cry out to You,
Then my enemies will turn back;
This I know, because God is for me.
In God (I will praise His word),
In the LORD (I will praise His word),
In God I have put my trust;
I will not be afraid.
What can man do to me?
Vows made to You are binding upon me, O God;
I will render praises to You,
For You have delivered my soul from death.
Have You not delivered my feet from falling,
That I may walk before God
In the light of the living?

*Mourners cried over a wineskin and put their
grief on display at the tomb. David, in the
Philistine's hands and in dire distress, asked the
Lord to put his tears in a bottle and write their
message in His book. Bottled bereavement,
arranged by angels and given to the King of
Heaven, is always recorded carefully, with*

Be Exalted, O God

Be merciful to me, O God, be merciful to me!
For my soul trusts in You;
And in the shadow of Your wings I will make
my refuge,
Until these calamities have passed by.
I will cry out to God Most High,
To God who performs all things for me.
He shall send from heaven and save me;
He reproaches the one who would
swallow me up.   Selah
God shall send forth His mercy and His truth.
My soul is among lions;
I lie among the sons of men who are set on fire,
Whose teeth are spears and arrows,
And their tongue a sharp sword.
Be exalted, O God, above the heavens;
Let Your glory be above all the earth.
They have prepared a net for my steps;
My soul is bowed down;
They have dug a pit before me;
Into the midst of it they themselves
have fallen.   Selah
My heart is steadfast, O God, my heart is steadfast;
I will sing and give praise.
Awake, my glory!
Awake, lute and harp!
I will awaken the dawn.
I will praise You, O Lord, among the peoples;
I will sing to You among the nations.
For Your mercy reaches unto the heavens,
And Your truth unto the clouds.
Be exalted, O God, above the heavens;
Let Your glory be above all the earth.

*Calamities force us to depend. Saul chased
David into the hills, not realizing he was
chasing him under God's wings.*
*When we think we have our backs to the wall
we shall discover a cave of comfort—and meet
our God within—ready to strengthen our
heart!—JB*

The Lord Judges Right

Do you indeed speak righteousness, you silent ones?
Do you judge uprightly, you sons of men?
No, in heart you work wickedness;
You weigh out the violence of your hands in the earth.
The wicked are estranged from the womb;
They go astray as soon as they are born,
speaking lies.
Their poison is like the poison of a serpent;
They are like the deaf cobra that stops its ear,
Which will not heed the voice of charmers,
Charming ever so skillfully.
Break their teeth in their mouth, O God!
Break out the fangs of the young lions, O LORD!
Let them flow away as waters which run continually;
When he bends his bow,
Let his arrows be as if cut in pieces.
Let them be like a snail which melts away as it goes,
Like a stillborn child of a woman,
that they may not see the sun.
Before your pots can feel the burning thorns,
He shall take them away as with a whirlwind,
As in His living and burning wrath.
The righteous shall rejoice when he sees
the vengeance;
He shall wash his feet in the blood of the wicked,
So that men will say,
"Surely there is a reward for the righteous;
Surely He is God who judges in the earth."

I have not suffered like the psalmist and therefore I cannot always feel as he feels or understand his reaction. But with him I rejoice that You, Lord, judge righteously, giving to each their due so that none can complain. In the final analysis, right will be rewarded and wrong will be punished, and that is eminently fair.—SB

I will praise You, O Lord, among the peoples;
I will sing to You among the nations.
For Your mercy reaches unto the heavens,
And Your truth unto the clouds.
Be exalted, O God, above the heavens;
Let Your glory be above all the earth.

The Lord Our Shield

Deliver me from my enemies, O my God;
Defend me from those who rise up against me.
Deliver me from the workers of iniquity,
And save me from bloodthirsty men.
For look, they lie in wait for my life;
The mighty gather against me, not for my
transgression nor for my sin, O Lord. They run
and prepare themselves through no fault of mine.
Awake to help me, and behold!
You therefore, O Lord God of hosts,
the God of Israel, awake to punish all the nations;
Do not be merciful to any wicked transgressors.
At evening they return, they growl like a dog,
And go all around the city.
Indeed, they belch out with their mouth;
Swords are in their lips; for they say, "Who hears?"
But You, O Lord, shall laugh at them;
You shall have all the nations in derision.
O You his Strength, I will wait for You.
For God is my defense;
My merciful God shall come to meet me;
God shall let me see my desire on my enemies.
Do not slay them, lest my people forget;
scatter them by Your power, and bring them down
O Lord our shield.
For the sin of their mouth and the words of their l
Let them even be taken in their pride,
And for the cursing and lying which they speak.
Consume them in wrath, consume them,
That they may not be;
And let them know that God rules in Jacob
To the ends of the earth.   Selah
. . . But I will sing of Your power; . . .
For You have been my defense
And refuge in the day of my trouble.
To You, O my Strength, I will sing praises;
For God is my defense, the God of my mercy.

*How precious is the dawn! How fresh are
the fragile colors the rising sun sends to
announce another day! How dark has
been the night, and how dreadful the
deeds of darkness! Awaken my soul with
the morning, Lord, and let me sing of
your protection during the night hours,
and allow me to praise You for the hope
with which You bathe my inner being.—SB*

You Have Been Angry

O God, You have cast us off;
You have broken us down;
You have been displeased;
Oh, restore us again!
You have made the earth tremble;
You have broken it;
Heal its breaches, for it is shaking.
You have shown Your people hard things;
You have made us drink the wine of confusion.
You have given a banner to those who fear You,
That it may be displayed because of the truth.   Selah
That Your beloved may be delivered,
Save with Your right hand, and hear me.
God has spoken in His holiness:
"I will rejoice;
I will divide Shechem
And measure out the Valley of Succoth.
Gilead is Mine, and Manasseh is Mine;
Ephraim also is the helmet for My head;
Judah is My lawgiver.
Moab is My washpot;
Over Edom I will cast My shoe;
Philistia, shout in triumph because of Me."
Who will bring me into the strong city?
Who will lead me to Edom?
Is it not You, O God, who cast us off?
And You, O God, who did not go out with our armies?
Give us help from trouble,
For vain is the help of man.
Through God we will do valiantly,
For it is He who shall tread down our enemies.

David had been fighting against Mesopotamia and Syria. Joab had helped the King to win a great victory in the Valley of Salt, and Samuel tells us David "got him a name" after this battle. The King, however, was more aware than ever that "vain is the help of man." When we've just won a big battle it's easy to forget it was "through God we did valiantly"! David remembered and we would do well to do the same.—JB

In the Shelter of Your Wings

Hear my cry, O God;
Attend to my prayer.
From the end of the earth I will cry to You,
When my heart is overwhelmed;
Lead me to the rock that is higher than I.
For You have been a shelter for me,
And a strong tower from the enemy.
I will abide in Your tabernacle forever;
I will trust in the shelter of Your wings.   Selah
For You, O God, have heard my vows;
You have given me the heritage of those who fear
Your name.
You will prolong the king's life,
His years as many generations.
He shall abide before God forever.
Oh, prepare mercy and truth, which may preserve him!
So I will sing praise to Your name forever,
That I may daily perform my vows.

*David "daily" performed his vows. Practicing a
daily discipline of praise and prayer made the
king a man after God's own heart. The king was
a high rock to Israel, but needed a "rock that is
higher than I"; strong, but needed a shelter and
a strong tower from his enemies; a protector of
the people, but needed God's wings to shelter
him, so daily he performed his vows to make
sure he remembered these things.—JB*

In God Alone

Truly my soul silently waits for God;
From Him comes my salvation.
He only is my rock and my salvation;
He is my defense; I shall not be greatly moved.
How long will you attack a man?
You shall be slain, all of you,
Like a leaning wall and a tottering fence.
They only consult to cast him down
from his high position;
They delight in lies; they bless with their mouth,
But they curse inwardly.   Selah
My soul, wait silently for God alone,
For my expectation is from Him.
He only is my rock and my salvation;
He is my defense;
I shall not be moved.
In God is my salvation and my glory;
The rock of my strength, and my refuge, is in God.
Trust in Him at all times, you people;
Pour out your heart before Him;
God is a refuge for us.   Selah
Surely men of low degree are a vapor,
Men of high degree are a lie;
If they are weighed in the balances,
They are altogether lighter than vapor.
Do not trust in oppression,
Nor vainly hope in robbery;
If riches increase, do not set your heart on them.
God has spoken once, twice I have heard this:
That power belongs to God.
Also to You, O Lord, belongs mercy;
For You render to each one according to his work.

At times I feel as insecure as a fence ready to fold—a wall about to collapse. And sometimes there are people around who apparently want to help my demise. But You, Lord, are strong on my behalf—not in an impersonal way, but in loving concern. This knowledge makes me strong.—SB

Longing for God

O God, You are my God; early will I seek You;
My soul thirsts for You; My flesh longs for You
In a dry and thirsty land where there is no water.
So I have looked for You in the sanctuary,
To see your power and Your glory.
Because Your lovingkindness is better than life,
My lips shall praise You.
Thus I will bless You while I live;
I will lift up my hands in Your name.
My soul shall be satisfied as with marrow and fatness,
And my mouth shall praise You with joyful lips.
When I remember You on my bed,
I meditate on You in the night watches.
Because You have been my help,
Therefore in the shadow of Your wings I will rejoice.
My soul follows close behind You;
Your right hand upholds me.
But those who seek my life, to destroy it,
Shall go into the lower parts of the earth.
They shall fall by the sword;
They shall be a portion for jackals.
But the king shall rejoice in God;
Everyone who swears by Him shall glory;
But the mouth of those who speak lies
shall be stopped.

There are times when things just don't seem to go right. Desires dry up, prospects become a wilderness, hope and aspiration turn to dust. The temptation to disgruntlement becomes severe, but that is the time to concentrate on You, Lord. Day or night I sing, I meditate, I rejoice in You—and the desert comes alive.—SB

Lord Protect Me

Hear my voice, O God, in my meditation;
Preserve my life from fear of the enemy.
Hide me from the secret counsel of the wicked,
From the insurrection of the workers of iniquity,
Who sharpen their tongue like a sword,
And bend their bows to shoot their arrows—
bitter words,
That they may shoot in secret at the blameless;
Suddenly they shoot at him and do not fear.
They encourage themselves in an evil matter;
They talk of laying snares secretly;
They say, "Who will see them?"
They devise iniquities:
"We have perfected a shrewd scheme."
Both the inward thought and the heart of man
are deep.
But God shall shoot at them with an arrow;
Suddenly they shall be wounded.
So He will make them stumble over their own tongue;
All who see them shall flee away.
All men shall fear,
And shall declare the work of God;
For they shall wisely consider His doing.
The righteous shall be glad in the LORD,
and trust in Him.
And all the upright in heart shall glory.

*James tells us, "if a man seems to be religious
but bridleth not his tongue—his religion is
vain." David talked of the tongues of his
enemies being like swords—their bitter words
like arrows. God knows the words in men's
mouths before they are uttered. He speaks and
evil tongues are silenced. He will lend us His
words of wisdom!—JB*

A God of Abundance

Praise is awaiting You, O God, in Zion;
And to You the vow shall be performed.
O You who hear prayer, to you all flesh will come.
Iniquities prevail against me;
As for our transgressions,
You will provide atonement for them.
Blessed is the man whom You choose,
And cause to approach You,
That he may dwell in Your courts.
We shall be satisfied with the goodness of Your house,
Of Your holy temple.
By awesome deeds in righteousness You will answer us,
O God of our salvation,
You who are the confidence of all the ends
of the earth,
And of the far-off seas;
Who established the mountains by His strength,
Being clothed with power;
You who still the noise of the seas,
The noise of their waves,
And the tumult of the peoples.
They also who dwell in the farthest parts
are afraid of Your signs;
You make the outgoings of the morning and evening
rejoice.
You visit the earth and water it,
You greatly enrich it;
The river of God is full of water;
You provide their grain, for so You have prepared it.
You water its ridges abundantly,
You settle its furrows;
You make it soft with showers, You bless its growth.
You crown the year with Your goodness,
And Your paths drip with abundance.
They drop on the pastures of the wilderness,
And the little hills rejoice on every side.
The pastures are clothed with flocks;
The valleys also are covered with grain;
They shout for joy, they also sing.

David has had a good year. His paths "drip with abundance." God has been his confidence; He has answered his prayers and He wants his world to know it. It is easy to stay near God when we suffer. It is much harder when we celebrate life. David was careful to share his blessings with others.—JB

You visit the earth and water it,
You greatly enrich it;
The river of God is full of water;
You provide their grain,
For so You have prepared it.

Let us Rejoice in God

Make a joyful shout to God, all the earth!
Sing out the honor of His name;
Make His praise glorious.
Say to God, "How awesome are Your works!
Through the greatness of Your power
Your enemies shall submit themselves to You.
All the earth shall worship You
And sing praises to You;
They shall sing praises to Your name."   Selah
Come and see the works of God;
He is awesome in His doing toward the sons of men.
He turned the sea into dry land;
They went through the river on foot.
There we will rejoice in Him.
He rules by His power forever;
His eyes observe the nations;
Do not let the rebellious exalt themselves.   Selah
Oh, bless our God, you peoples!
And make the voice of His praise to be heard,
Who keeps our soul among the living,
And does not allow our feet to be moved.
For You, O God, have proved us;
You have refined us as silver is refined.
You brought us into the net;
You laid affliction on our backs.
You have caused men to ride over our heads;
We went through fire and through water;
But You brought us out to rich fulfillment.

[verses 1–12]

Sparkling waters, shimmering sunlight,
towering palms, rustling fronds, and awesome
clouds combine to touch me in the depths of my
soul. The beauty, the symmetry, and unity
speak mysteriously to me and elevate me. They
point me to You, Lord, as they in their
inanimate way praise You. And I view them in
my way—the special way in which only
redeemed humanity can adequately praise
You.—SB

Praise Him

I will go into Your house with burnt offerings;
I will pay You my vows,
which my lips have uttered
And my mouth has spoken when I was in trouble.
I will offer You burnt sacrifices of fat animals,
With the sweet aroma of rams;
I will offer bulls with goats.   Selah
Come and hear, all you who fear God,
And I will declare what He has done for my soul.
I cried to Him with my mouth,
And He was extolled with my tongue.
If I regard iniquity in my heart,
The Lord will not hear.
But certainly God has heard me;
He has attended to the voice of my prayer.
Blessed be God,
Who has not turned away my prayer,
Nor His mercy from me!

[verses 13–20]

There have been times of extremity when I called to You, Lord. It wasn't a usual calling—from the depths I spoke to You. I made promises—and so did You. Now it's time to say "thanks" and to testify to other people about Your faithfulness. What a privilege, having spoken to You, now to be able to speak of You!—SB

Benediction

God be merciful to us and bless us,
And cause His face to shine upon us.   Selah
That Your way may be known on earth,
Your salvation among all nations.
Let the peoples praise You, O God;
Let all the peoples praise You.
Oh, let the nations be glad and sing for joy!
For You shall judge the people righteously,
And govern the nations on earth.   Selah
Let the peoples praise You, O God;
Let all the peoples praise You.
Then the earth shall yield her increase;
God, our own God, shall bless us.
God shall bless us,
And all the ends of the earth shall fear Him.

When God's face shines, blessing comes. When God's face is dark, we rightly tremble. God's smile lights up our lives; God's frown leaves us cold and afraid. God "always" smiles upon His Son. When He sees Christ in our lives, God's face shines—and our souls are warmed!—JB

My soul, wait silently for God alone,
for my expectation is from Him.
He only is my rock and my salvation;
He is my defense; I shall not be moved.
In God is my salvation and my glory;
The rock of my strength, and my refuge is in God.
Trust Him at all times, you people; pour out your
heart before Him;
God is a refuge for us.

I will praise You, O Lord, among the peoples;
I will sing to You among the nations.
For Your mercy reaches unto the heavens,
And Your truth unto the clouds.
Be exalted, O God, above the heavens;
Let Your glory be above all the earth.